JAVA PROGI

Your Step by Step Guide to
Easily Learn Java in 7 Days

iCode Academy

JAVA FOR BEGINNERS

document, including, but not limited to, — errors, omissions, or inaccuracies.

Table of Contents

Introduction

The world of programming is a very diverse one where each programming language has its own specific advantages. There are languages such as C and Assembly which focus on operating system instructions and other computer software while there are other languages such as HTML and JavaScript which focus on web-based applications. An example of a programming language that can do both is Java. This eBook contains guides and instructions that will help you learn and understand java in one day.

So what is Java?

Java is actually a decent programming language developed at Sun Microsystems. It was originally used for Internet applications or *applets*. Those applets are embedded on web pages and run in the browser. Java uses a special format known as *byte code* instead of an ordinary machine code. With the help of a Java interpreter program, the byte code can be executed on any computer. This Java interpreter program is called a Java Virtual Machine or JVM. It is available today in most computer systems. Java may use byte code format but there is nothing about Java that requires this byte code technique. There are some compilers that exist and generate real machine code, or more commonly known as native code.

Java programs consist of sets of classes. The source files of those programs are written in .java. These source files are then compiled into .class files which contain the byte code instead of the CPU-specific machine code. The .class files are then executed by a Java Virtual Machine (JVM or interpreter) at run time.

Java is not limited to Internet applications. It is technically a complete general object-oriented programming language which can be used to develop all sorts of applications. The syntax of Java is very much similar to the syntax of C++ but removes its error-prone features and complications.

Do not mistake Java for JavaScript. JavaScript is an entirely different language. JavaScript is an interpreted programming language used as one of the three essential components of a webpage or website content production. The difference between Java and JavaScript is that Java is an object-oriented programming language while JavaScript is an object-oriented-scripting language. Codes written in Java need to be compiled while the codes written in JavaScript are all in text. Java creates applications that can run in both a virtual machine and a browser while JavaScript can only run on a browser. Each language also requires different sets of plug-ins.

Sun Microsystems, the company behind the creation of Java, offer free tools for developing Java-based software. If you want to know more about those tools, you can visit this website (https://www.java.sun.com) for more information such as Java compilers for different computer systems (UNIX, Microsoft Windows, OSX) along with detailed documentation. Java compilers are free and can be down-loaded from the given link.

Throughout the eBook, we will discuss the basics of how Java programs are compiled, simple expressions and declarations, classes, objects, and statements, until you are able to learn, understand, and write a complete Java program in just one day.

Chapter 1:
Basics of Java

Compiling and running a Java Program

Every source file in Java contains exactly one class. The filename must be the same as the class name. For example, a class **Hello** should be stored in the source file **Hello.java**. Using the **javac** compiler, the source file Hello.java can be compiled in the terminal:

javac Hello.java

This will result in a file with the same name as the source file but a different file extension; the .class extension. The class file now contains the byte code. This means that it cannot be executed immediately. It needs a Java Virtual Machine or byte code interpreter:

java Hello

The command above loads and executes the Hello class and its main method. If the class contains extensions from other classes (to be discussed further on the following chapters), these classes are loaded automatically when needed. If you have a source file which extends several other source files, you can compile all of them using:

javac *.java

Assuming that all files are in the same folder, each source file will load and execute its corresponding class file.

Declarations and Expressions

There are eight primitive types in Java. By primitive, it means that these types are not defined in terms of anything else; basically, atomic. They are sequences of bits that the CPU is ready to deal with. These types are:

Byte, short, int, long, float, double, char, Boolean

If a variable type is not a primitive type, it is considered a **reference type**. A reference type can either be a class, interface, or array type. A variable of any reference type can be set to **null**. This means that it can hold nothing

Java supports the usual set of data types such as integer, char, boolean, and other variables. Here are some:

> **int** a, b; //integer variables
> **float** f; //float variable
> **char** s; //character variable
> boolean a; //returns true or false

Note: "//" and "/* */" are used to serve for single line comments and multiple line comments respectively.

Numerical expressions can be written in pretty much the same way as other languages.

> a = 2 * (3 + 1);
> b = c / 4.12643;
> p = q % 2;
> o = **true;**
> s = 'L';

It is possible to assign an initial value to a variable directly when declaring it.

> int a = 5;
> float f = 0.52;

The division operator in Java actually means two different things. It can either be real division for real numbers, or integer division for integers. This is not really a problem in most cases although it may lead to varying results.

```
double a;
a = 1 / 9; // the result of a will be 0.0
a = 1.0 / 9.0; // the result of a will be 0.111...
```

The first operation performed integer division, hence the result of 0. If you want to get the exact quotient of 1 and 9, you need to express 1 and 9 as real values so that the division becomes real division.

It is possible in java to assign a real value to an integer variable. The value is automatically converted to the corresponding type. This is called **typecasting**.

Java supports type conversion (typecasting) but does not perform the conversions automatically. The programmer is required to indicate where and what conversions must be made by writing the desired type in parentheses before the expression.

```
double a;
int b;
b = (int) (a * 12.3223122);
```

Of course, it is possible to assign an integer value to a real variable without typecasting. It is not necessary to cast as long as the conversion can be performed without the loss of any information.

Java is an object-oriented programming language, so the terms that we will use are a little different compared to terms used in structural programming languages.

Functions, sub-routines, and procedures in Java are called *methods*. The term used for calling or executing a function is called *invoking*. A collection of variables and methods put together is called a *class*.

Here are some examples of methods:

```
Class HelloWorld{
public void sayHi(int a, int b){
aa = a;
bb = b;
}
```

```
private int getAge(){
return x;
}
}
```

The example above contains two methods: sayHi and getAge. A method can have multiple parameters or none.

Notice that one method begins with the keyword public and the second one begins with private? This indicates whether the method can be accessed from other classes or not. This is helpful when you are securing some data that should not be accessed by other methods.

Similar to the <u>struct</u> type in C (record structure), variables in Java are considered as a group for every instance of the class. An *object* is considered an occurrence of the struct or record.

In other words, an *object* is an *instance* of its class.

Knowing what the class of an object is also means knowing what set of variables it has and what methods it can perform. It may sound odd because a set of variables cannot supposedly perform anything. This is the **core** of object-oriented programming. It means that every code is considered as being executed by an object.

Here is an example of a simple Java code:

```
Class Section{ //This is defining a class called "Section"
int a, b, c; //These are three integer instance variables declared
/*every Section instance will have its own values for these variable */
void add(int aa, int bb, int cc){
a+= aa; //this adds (aa, bb) to (a, b)
b+=bb;
this.c += cc //"this.c" is the same as "c"
}
}
```

Now you're probably wondering what the "this" was for. Well, every method in a class contains a secret unlisted argument which is the group of variables. That argument is this. The method add needs to know which section it is adding. The caller needs to tell which section to add. Any call to add needs to be linked to a specific instance of the Hello class.

```
Section s1;
s1 = new Section();
s1.a = 1;
s1.b = p.x * 2;
s1.c = 0
s1.add(1,2,3);
```

The last line of code above means that whenever translate is called, the argument this will be equal to p1.

If the object performing a method is not specified, it is safe to assume that this should perform the method.

In other words:

```
add(1, 2, 3 );
```

can be considered the same as

```
this.add(1, 2, 3);
```

We will discuss methods, objects and classes in more detail in chapters 3 to 4. For now, look at the example of a simple Java program:

```
public class HelloWorld{

public static void main(String[] args){
System.out.print("Hello World!"); //this prints out "Hello World"

} //main
} //HelloWorld
```

The code above is a simple Java program which prints out "Hello World!"

Let's try to discuss the lines of code one by one.

First you'll see the class declaration HelloWorld. The public indication denotes that it can be accessed by other classes.

Second, we'll see the method main. Notice the new word "static" on the method declaration? This simply means that when the method is called, it is not associated with an object but with the class itself. In other words, the method cannot access any attributes.

Third is the "args" parameter. This parameter gets the value of the data from the information other than the class name executed by the Java interpreter, if there are any.

Note: The System.out.print is a method that displays what the programmer writes inside the quotations marks

(" "). If you want to print out a new line when running, you can use System.out.println. This will make a new line for displaying the output.

Example #2:

```java
import java.util.Scanner; //import package
public class User{

  public static void main( String[] args ){

Scanner inp = new Scanner(System.in); //declaration of a new object Scanner

  String f_name; //string variable declarations

String l_name;
String full_name;

  System.out.print("Enter your first name:"); //this line here asks for your first
  name

  f_name = inp.next(); //the input you type in will be stored in f_name via
  inp.next()

System.out.print("Enter your last name:"); //this line on the other hand, asks for
your last name

  l_name = inp.next(); //the input you type in will now be stored in l_name

  full_name = f_name + " " + l_name; //this line here stores both f_name and
  l_name in full_name while being seperated by " "

  System.out.println("Hello,"+ full_name + "! Pleased to meet you."); //This
  line prints out your full_name.
```

```
}//main
}//User
```

Now, the code above is an example of a basic input-output program in Java. First, let's try to discuss what the line import java.util.Scanner; means. The Scanner class is a class that is really helpful when handling user input. To use the Scanner class, we need to reference it to our code via the keyword import. Import is basically the same as the #include in C. This means that import references external libraries that are ready to use for our program.

Next is the line Scanner inp = new Scanner(System.in);

This line simply creates an object instance of the method Scanner. The System.in denotes that it will store the input given by a user.

```
f_name = inp.next();
l_name = inp.next();
```

The two lines of code above demonstrate how the input will be stored in f_name and l_name respectively. The line inp.next(); means that whatever input the user types in next, it will be stored in the corresponding variable assigned to it.

The line full_name = f_name + " " + l_name; The + symbols after f_name and before l_name indicate that you could put a defined string or character in between. The + symbols simply connect both user inputs and characters or symbols in one line or statement.

Chapter 2:
Conditional Statements, Iterative Statements, and Branching Statements

Statements in Java can be written in the same manner as in other languages. Similar to how statements are written in C or Pascal, these statements can be grouped together in sections using '{'and '}'.

If-then-else Statement

Like almost all languages, the if-then-else statement in Java allows an alternate path of execution when the "if" condition evaluates to false. Here is an example:

```
void isZero() {
If( x == 0 ) {
System.out.println("x is zero.");
}

  System.out.println("X is not equal to zero.");

}
```

Just like other languages, it is possible in Java to have an if-statement alone. You can have just the if-statement if your code does not have a lot of conditional executions.

Now, take a look at the following code:

```
Import Java.util.Scanner;
Class ConditionCheck {
Public static void main ( String[] args ) {
int grade;
Scanner sc = new Scanner( );
System.out.print.ln("Enter your grade (0 – 100):");
number = sc.next();
if (grade == 100) {

  System.out.println(" You had a perfect score! Congratulations!");
```

```
} else if (grade >= 60) {

System.out.println("You passed the exam with a score of " + grade + "%.");

} else if (grade < 60 ) {

System.out.println("You failed the exam. You should study more to pass the
next one.");

}
}
}
```

The program above demonstrates a simple grade checker. Just like any other language, Java can have multiple conditional statements. The ConditionCheck class is an example of one. The program will output "You had a perfect score" if the user input is equal to 100. If the user input is greater than or equal to 60, the program will output "You passed the exam with a score of (grade) %" but if the user input is less than 60, the program will output "You failed the exam. You should study more to pass the next one.

Boolean Expressions

Boolean expressions can be used with logical operators corresponding to 'and', 'or', and 'not'. These operators are written in Java as:

```
And | &&
Or | ||
Not | !
```

Here is an example:

```
If(a == 0 && b!=a) {
B++;
}
```

Switch-Case Statement

Although the switch statement is also a conditional statement like if-then and if-then-else, it differs through a number of varieties. A switch statement works with primitive data types such as byte, short, char, and int. Switch statements also work with enumerated data-types such as string and a few special classes that cover certain primitive types like char, byte, short, and int~in other words, a record.

```java
public class SwitchCase {
public static void main(String[] args) {
int month = 8;
String monthStr;
switch (month) {

  case 1: monthStr = "January";
  break;
  case 2: monthStr = "February";
  break;
  case 3: monthStr = "March";
  break;
  case 4: monthStr = "April";
  break;
  case 5: monthStr = "May";
  break;
  case 6: monthStr = "June";
  break;
  case 7: monthStr = "July";
  break;
  case 8: monthStr = "August";
  break;
  case 9: monthStr = September";
  break;
  case 10: monthStr = "October";
  break;
  case 11: monthStr = "November";
  break;
  case 12: monthStr = "December";
  break;
  default: monthStr = "Invalid month";
  break;

}
System.out.println(monthStr);
```

```
}
}
```

The code above demonstrates how a switch statement is written in Java. Note that the value of int month is 8 and there are 13 cases written including a default case to check if the value of month is (not) an integer between 1 and 12. Considering the value of int month is, the result of the println will be 'August'.

The difference between if-else statement and switch statement is that the switch statement is much easier to read. Imagine having many multiple conditions written in if-else. It will be difficult to write and also hard to read.

Another difference is the keyword break. In an if-else, the program only goes to one condition block at a time while in a switch statement; the program can go through all cases sequentially. Here is an example:

```
int month = 8;
switch (month) {
case 1: System.out.println(" January ");
case 2: System.out.println(" February ");
case 3: System.out.println(" March ");
case 4: System.out.println(" April ");
case 5: System.out.println(" May ");
case 6: System.out.println(" June ");
case 7: System.out.println(" July ");
case 8: System.out.println(" August ");
case 9: System.out.println(" September ");
case 10: System.out.println(" October ");
case 11: System.out.println(" November ");
case 12: System.out.println(" December ");
break;
default: break;
}
```

Since the value of month is 8, the condition will jump to case 8 and that the break line is only written after case 12. The resulting output of the code will be:

August

September

October

November

December

Switch Statements and Strings

In the Java SE 7 and later versions of Java SE, it is possible to use the String data type in switch statements. Here is an example:

```java
public class getDate {
public static int getMonthNo(String month) {
int monthNo = 0;
if (month == null) {
return monthNo;
}
switch ( month.toLowerCase() ) {
case "january" : monthNo = 1;
break;
case "february" : monthNo = 2;
break;
case "march" : monthNo = 3;
break;
case "april" : monthNo = 4;
break;
case "may" : monthNo = 5;
break;
case "june" : monthNo = 6;
break;
case "july" : monthNo = 7;
break;
case "august" : monthNo = 8;
break;
case "september": monthNo = 9;
break;
case "october" : monthNo = 10;
break;
case "november": monthNo = 11;
break;
case "december": monthNo = 12;
```

```
break;
default: monthNo = 0;
break;
}
return monthNo; }
public static void main (String[] args) {
String month = "August";
int returnedMonthNo = StringSwitchDemo.getMonthNo(month);
if (returnedMonthNo == 0) {
System.out.println( " Invalid month");
} else {
System.out.println(returnedMonthNo);
}
}
}
```

The output of the code above is 8. The String data type in the switch expression is compared with the expressions linked with each case label like as if the String = method were being used. The value of the variable month needs to be converted to lowercase using the .toLowerCase method so that the getDate class example to be able to accept any month regardless of case. All the strings associated with the case label are in lowercase.

Note: The code above also checks whether the expression in the switch statement has a value of null. It is important to remember that the expression in any switch statement is not null in order to prevent a NullPointerException from having an error or being thrown.

Loops and Iterative Statements
The While Statement

The while statement in Java is pretty much not that different from the while statements of other programming languages. The while statement continuously executes a section of instructions while the condition indicated is true. It's syntax can be written as:

```
while (expression | instruction| condition) {
Statement | instruction | condition (s);
}
```

The while statement checks the expression which needs to return a boolean value. As long as the value of the expression evaluates to true, the while statement will continue the instructions or statements included inside the while section. The while statement will continue evaluating the expression and will execute its instructions until the value of the expression becomes false. The sample code below prints out the values from 1 to 10 given the expression **count.**

```
class displayNumbers {
public static void main(String[] args){
int count = 1;
while (count < 11) {
System.out.println ("Count is: " + count);
count++;
}
}
}
```

As you can see in the code above, the while statement checks if the value of count is not greater than 11. If the expression evaluates to true, the program will enter the while-statement and execute the line System.out.println("Count is:" + count) ;.

After that, the value of count will be increased and re-evaluate its value until the expression count < 11 becomes false.

It is also possible to implement an infinite loop using the while statement. The sample code below demonstrates how:

```
while (true){
// your code goes here
}
```

Since the expression will always evaluate to true, the while statement will keep executing the instructions inside the block; hence, the infinite loop.

Do-while Statement

In the Java programming language, there is also a do-while statement. The do-while statement does not really have that much of a difference when compared to the do-while statements of other programming languages.

The do-while statement can be expressed like this:

```
do {
statement(s)
} while (expression);
```

When the program enters the do-while statement, it immediately executes the instructions and statements inside the block. After that will it only check if the expression is true or not.

What's the difference between a do-while and a while?

The difference between do-while and while is that do-while evaluates its expression at the bottom of the loop instead of the top. Therefore, the statements within the do block are always executed at least once.

The code below demonstrates how a Java program with a simple do-while loop works:

```
class DoWhileSample {
public static void main(String[] args){
int count = 1;
do {
System.out.println("Count is: " + count);
count++;
} while (count < 11);
}}
```

For Statement

In the Java Programming Language, thefor statement gives an accurate task to loop or iterate over a range of values. A common term used by developers and programmers for the for statement is the "for loop" due to its repetitive iteration until its conditions and expressions are met.

A for loop can be written as:

```
for (initial value; terminating condition; incrementing value) {
```

```
//expressions | statements| methods
}
```

In using a for loop, it is vital to note that the initial value is the starting point of the loop. It is only executed once; at the beginning. Once the terminating condition is met, the loop will halt and terminate the iteration. If the terminating condition is not yet met, every time the loop iterates, the incrementing value is added to the current value of the expression. It will keep incrementing as long as the terminating condition evaluates to true. The incrementing value can also be decrementing depending on the flow of the program.

```
class sample_For {
public static void main(String[] args){
for (int x=1; x<10; x++){
System.out.println ("The current value of the count is: " + x);
}
}
}
```

The example code above shows the common use of a for loop in Java. The output of the program will be:

```
The current value of the count is: 1
The current value of the count is: 2
The current value of the count is: 3
The current value of the count is: 4
The current value of the count is: 5
The current value of the count is: 6
The current value of the count is: 7
The current value of the count is: 8
The current value of the count is: 9
```

If you'll notice, the code declares variable within the expression. The scope of the loop covers the declaration of the variable up to the end of the loop section for that it can be useful in terminating and incrementing the expression. If the variable inside the loop is not needed elsewhere, it is a better practice to just declare the variable inside the loop in order to reduce errors.

The expressions inside the for loop are not required. In other words, if the program enters the for loop and there are no expressions present, there will be nothing to evaluate. This will result to an infinite loop as seen in the sample code below.

```
for ( ; ; ) {
//procedures / codes / statements
}
```

There is an alternate way of writing a for loop. This form is useful when iterating through arrays and records (to be discussed in chapter 3). Other terms for this form of for loop is an *enhanced for statement*. The enhanced for statement is useful in making loops more compressed and readable. Here is an example code applying an enhanced for loop in arrays:

```
class EnhancedForExample {
public static void main(String[] args){
int[] values =
{11, 12, 13, 14, 15, 16, 17, 18, 19, 20};
for (int list : numbers ) {
System.out.println("The number is : " + list);
}
}
}
```

The loop in the code looks a bit different from a normal for loop. The variable list functions like a pointer to the current index and allows access to its current value. The output of the program above will be:

```
The number is : 11
The number is : 12
The number is : 13
The number is : 14
The number is : 15
The number is : 16
The number is : 17
The number is : 18
The number is : 19
The number is : 20
```

The use of the enhanced for statement is recommended especially when handling arrays and records. It reduces the possibility of iteration errors and improves the readability of the code.

Branching Statements

The Break Statement

We've all seen how the break statement works. Once a program encounters a break statement, it terminates the code section it is included in. Indeed, this is the most common application of break. Another application is a break with label. Although it is almost the same as an unlabeled break, the term *label* makes the difference. Here is a sample code:

```
public class Hello{
public static void main(String[] args){
int x,y;
loop:
for(x=0;x<5;x++){
System.out.println(" ");
for(y=0;y<5;y++){
System.out.print("x ");
if(y==3 && x==2 ){
break loop;
}}}}}
```

By adding a statement "loop", a labeled break becomes possible. Based on the code above, when the value of y evaluates to 3 and the value of evaluates to 2, the break statement with terminate the section covered by the label loop. The result of the program above is:

```
x x x x x
x x x x x
 x x x x
```

Continue Statement

The continue statement is actually the opposite of the break statement. It is the opposite in a sense that it *keeps a section running* if the conditions inside the expression evaluate to true. It is not entirely opposite though since it skips the current iteration of the for, while, and do-while loops.

Like the break statement, the continue statement has an unlabeled and labeled form. In an unlabeled continue statement, the expression is evaluated so that the program will know if it should skip to the end of the code section. Here is an example of an unlabeled continue statement:

```java
public class Hello{
public static void main(String[] args){
int x,y;
for(x=0;x<5;x++){
System.out.println(" ");
for(y=0;y<5;y++){
System.out.print("x ");
if(y==3 && x==2 ){
continue;
}}}}}
```

The output of the code above will be:

```
x x x x x
x x x x x
x x x x x
x x x x x
x x x x x
```

Note: Since the code above is an unlabeled continue statement, the code will not skip the expression included although it will still evaluate whether the expression is true of false.

A labeled continue, on the other hand, skips the loop where the label begins. Here is an example of a labeled continue statement:

```
public class Hello{
public static void main(String[] args){
int x,y;
loop:
for(x=0;x<5;x++){
System.out.println(" ");
for(y=0;y<5;y++){
System.out.print("x ");
if(y==3 && x==2 ){
continue loop;
}
}
}
}
}
```

The output of the program will be:

```
x x x x x
x x x x x
 x x x x
x x x x x
x x x x x
```

Notice the third row does not have 5 x's? That's because when the expression if (y == 3 && x == 2) became true, the continue label jumped right back to the loop for (x = 0; x < 5; x ++). This means that the continue statement skipped when the program arrived when the expression if(y == 3 && x == 2) became true. That is what a labeled continue statement does.

The return Statement

The return statement is different from both the break and continue statements. It exits from a method and returns to where the method was called.

A return statement, like the return statement in other programming languages, has two forms: one that returns a value, and one that does not. In order to return a value, simply write the value or expression that evaluates the value after the return keyword. Here is an example:

```
return answer;
```

Here is an example of a return statement without a value:

```
return;
```

Note: When a return statement is used, the return type of the method should be int. If void is declared for a method, the return statement will not work. The data type after the return value must also be the same as the one declared as a parameter in the method. Otherwise, the program will run into an error.

We will see more use of the return statement on chapter 4.

Chapter 3:
Arrays

An array is not a primitive data type in Java. It is, in other words, a collection of variables of the same data type; basically a container. It holds a number of values of the same data type. The size of an array is always fixed. Once an array has been created, it cannot be expanded.

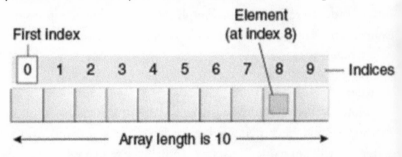

As you can see in the image above, the positions in an array are called *indices* or *index*. The values stored in those indices are called elements. If you noticed, the beginning of the array starts an index 0 and ends at index 9. Arrays in java are pretty much the same from other programming languages.

Array Declaration

Consider an integer variable sample_array. In order to make the sample_array an array of integer, add [ ] after the int. Here is an example:

int[ ] sample_array;

You have just declared an array of integers named sample_array. Now, an array declaration can be split into two components: the datatype of the array and the name of the array itself. Based on the example above, the datatype of the array is int[ ] and the name of the array is sample_array. The [ ] remain empty because they are not a part of the data type. It just signifies that you are declaring the variable as an array. Although you have declared the array, it does not mean you have created one.

Note: Like any other variable, declaring the array properly is very important. Otherwise, your program will run into a compilation error.

Java arrays are not restricted to integer arrays. Here are some examples of other types of arrays in Java:

```
String[] string_array_sample;
byte[] byte_array_sample;
long[] long_array_sample;
float[] float_array_sample;
boolean[] boolean_array_sample;
double[] double_array_sample;
char[] char_array_sample;
short[] short_array_sample;
```

The following lines of code are examples of how to assign values (elements) to specific array indices:

```
sample_array [ 0 ] = 24;
char_array_sample[ 4 ] = "E";
```

In order to access an array and display it, the name of the array and the index of the element that you want to access can be used:

```
System.out.println ("The value is: " + sample_array [ 0 ] );
System.out.println ("The element is: " + char_array_sample [ 4 ] );
System.out.println ("The element in the index is " + sample_array [ 5 ] + ".");
```

Another way of declaring your array can be done like in the following code:

```
int[ ] sample_array = {
20,444, 195,
23, 0, 100,
32, 55, 19,
10, 14, 123,
150, 141, 170
};
```

Using the way above to declare an array, the size of the array can easily be determined since the number of elements between the curly braces is known.

Placing the brackets after the array name is also accepted when declaring an array. Here is an example:

```
int test_array[ ];
char array_char[ ];
```

Although this is acceptable, it is not a good practice since the brackets are the ones that identify the array type. They should appear beside the data type.

Take a look at the following program:

```
public class simple_array{
public static void main(String[ ] args){
int[ ] sample_array;
sample_array = new int [10];
sample_array[0] = 23;
sample_array[1] = 12;
sample_array[2] = 33;
sample_array[3] = 42;
sample_array[4] = 56;
sample_array[5] = 77;
sample_array[6] = 99;
sample_array[7] = 11;
sample_array[8] = 53;
sample_array[9] = 66;
System.out.println (" The element for index 0 = "+ sample_array[0] );
System.out.println (" The element for index 1 = "+ sample_array[1] );
System.out.println (" The element for index 2 = "+ sample_array[2] );
System.out.println (" The element for index 3 = "+ sample_array[3] );
System.out.println (" The element for index 4 = "+ sample_array[4] );
System.out.println (" The element for index 5 = "+ sample_array[5] );
System.out.println (" The element for index 6 = "+ sample_array[6] );
System.out.println (" The element for index 7 = "+ sample_array[7] );
System.out.println (" The element for index 8 = "+ sample_array[8] );
System.out.println (" The element for index 9 = "+ sample_array[9] );
}
```

The output of the Java code above will be: The element for index =

The element for index 0 = 23
The element for index 1 = 12
The element for index 2 = 33

The element for index 3 = 42

The element for index 4 = 56

The element for index 5 = 77

The element for index 6 = 99

The element for index 7 = 11

The element for index 8 = 53

The element for index 9 = 66

If you'll notice, it is rather tiresome and difficult to declare all the elements of an array. Imagine having 100 elements that you need to print out or store. Wouldn't writing them one by one be troublesome? In most cases, programmers implement iterative statements (while, do-while, and for) to make the iteration through each element in the array much simpler.

Here is an example of an array implementation using loops:

```
public class loop_array {
public static void main (String[ ] args) {
int x = 10;
int [ ] sample_array;
sample_array = new int [ x ];
for ( x = 0; x < 10; x ++ ){
sample_array [ x ] = x;
System.out.println(" The element of index " + x + " is " + sample_array [ x ] +".");
}
}
}
```

The output of the code above will be:

The element of index 0 is 0.

The element of index 1 is 1.

The element of index 2 is 2.

The element of index 3 is 3.

The element of index 4 is 4.

The element of index 5 is 5.

The element of index 6 is 6.

The element of index 7 is 7.

The element of index 8 is 8.

The element of index 9 is 9.

Examine the code properly. You'll notice that the size of the array was set to x whose value is 10. You'll also see that instead of declaring the elements one by one, a for loop was written to iterate the storing and printing of all the elements of the array. The for loop goes through each index and stores the current value of x as it increments and goes on to the next index.

It is also possible in Java to declare an array of arrays or in other terms, a multi-dimensional array. A multidimensional array can be made by adding two or more sets of brackets after the data type instead of adding just one. Each element in the array can be accessed by a specific combination of index values.

Multi-dimensional arrays in Java are a bit different from the multi-dimensional arrays in C or other languages since the components of the multi-dimensional array in java are also arrays.

To be able to understand that more, here is a sample code:

```
class sample_md_array {
public static void main(String[] args) {
String[][] rankings = {
{"Sgt. ", "Lt. ", "Capt. "},
{"John", "Maximus"}
};
System.out.println(rankings[0][0] + names[1][0]);
System.out.println(rankings[0][1] + names[1][1]);
}
}
```

The output from the code will be:

```
Sgt. John
Lt. Maximus
```

Now, since we can declare the elements of an array, we can now use the built-in length attribute in order to know the size of any array. To do that, we can write:

```
System.out.println(sample_array.length);
```

This will print out the number of elements in an array.

Array Replication

Java has a built-in method from the class System that can be used to copy data from one array to another. That method is called arraycopy. Here is an example:

```
public static void arraycopy(Object src, int srcPos,
Object dest, int destPos, int length)
```

The objects src and dest determine the array source and the array destination. In other words, src means the array where the data will be copied from and dest means the array where the data will be copied to. The srcPos determines the starting position or starting index where the arraycopy method will begin. The destPos functions the same as srcPos but determines the starting position in the destination array. The integer length determines how many elements the programmer wants to copy.

Look at the following sample program arr_copy_sample:

```
class arr_copy_sample{
public static void main(String[] args) {
int[] sourceArr = { 0, 2, 4, 6, 8, 10, 12, 14, 16 };
int[] destArr = new int[7];
int x;
System.arraycopy(sourceArr, 1, destArr, 0, 7);
for(x = 0; x < 7; x++){
System.out.print(destArr[x] + " ");
}
}
}
```

The output from this program is:

```
2 4 6 8 10 12 14 16
```

Array Element Manipulation

In the world of programming the use of arrays can be a very powerful and efficient concept. In Java SE, there are some methods that enable the programmer to perform some of the most common manipulation methods in arrays. One example is the arr_copy_sample class. The method arraycopy in the sample code utilizes the the class System instead of manually looping through each and every single of the elements of the source array and replicating each one to the destination array. This process takes place during program runtime. It just enables the developer to use the code to invoke the method.

To avoid manual iteration and provide convenience, Java SE offers some methods for manipulating arrays. These methods include common procedures such as copying, searching and sorting the arrays. The java.util.Arrays class provides those methods. One example can be applied to the arr_copy_sample code.

```
class Hello{
public static void main(String[] args) {
int[] sourceArr = { 0, 2, 4, 6, 8, 10, 12, 14, 16 };
int x;
int [] destArr = java.util.Arrays.copyOfRange(sourceArr, 1, 8);
for(x = 0; x < 7; x++){
System.out.print(destArr[x] + " ");
}
}
}
```

If you'll notice, a method copyOfRange from the java.util.Arrays package was used instead of the arraycopy method. Its difference is that the developer is no longer required to initialize the destination array before invoking the method since the destination array itself is the value returned by the method.

The output of the program will also be the same as the program which applied the arraycopy method but if you'll examine more properly, the starting index to be copied to the destination array is no longer required. Only the source array, the starting index and up to what index the method needs to reach; in other words, the final index to be copied.

Other methods that the java.util.Arrays package class include are:

BinarySearch method

- This method searches the array for a specific value by locating the index where it is placed.

Equals Method

- This method compares two arrays in order to determine if the values are equal or not.

Fill method

- This method is used for storing values. It fills the array by placing a specific value at each index.

ParallelSort

- This method was only introduced in Java SE 8. The parallelSort arranges the elements concurrently of an array into ascending order. Parallel sorting is very efficient in arranging large amounts of arrays; typically on multiprocessor systems.

Sort Method

- This method also works the same as the parallelSort method but sorts the elements of the array sequentially.

Chapter 4:
Methods, Objects, Classes

We have already had a short introduction about classes, methods, and objects in the previous chapters. In this chapter, we will discuss these terms in more detail.

Classes

A class is generally a declaration which contains a specific set of attributes or in other words, instance variables. Together with methods, declaring a Java class can be very much similar to declaring one in Simula.

Take a look at the following code:

```
Class Example{
Private int value;
Protected char letter;
}
```

If you'll notice, there are declarations right before the data types int and char. These declarations mean that the attributes cannot be accessed outside of the class. Overall, attributes need to remain private or protected in order to prevent direct unauthorized access from other classes. There are three declarations normally used in Java: private, protected and public.

Public

- This declaration means the attribute can be accessed from other classes.

Private

- This declaration does not allow the attribute to be accessed by any other class except its own.

Protected

- This class is somewhat similar to a private declaration although it gives access to its own class and its subclasses but not classes from the outside.

A class in Java is defined like this:

```
class MyOwnClass {
// field, constructor, and
// method declarations
}
```

The code above is an example of how to write a class declaration. The area between the curly braces is called the class body. It contains pretty much the codes that initialize the objects made from the class. These codes include:

Constructors, declarations, methods

We are already familiar with declarations and methods. Let's talk about the constructors. Constructors are used to create new objects. A class can contain constructors which are executed to create objects from the main class.

In appearance, declaring constructors is almost the same as declaring methods except for two things: Constructors use the name of the class and do not have a return type.

Here is an example of a constructor of class Example:

```
public class Example{
int start;
int final;
int middle;
//constructor
public Example(int Constart, int Confinal, int Conmiddle ) {
start = Constart;
final = confinal;
middle = Conmiddle;
}
}
```

The following code shows how to create a new Example object called samp:

Example samp = new Example(0, 10, 5);

The code new Example (0, 10, 5) creates space in the memory for initializing the object and its values.

Arguments in a constructor are not required. For example:

```
Public Example ( ) {
Int start = 0;
Int final = 10;
Int middle = 5;
}
```

Creating the object is also the same but without the parameters:

```
samp Example = new Example ( );
```

Both constructors can be declared in class Example since the arguments they have are different. Just like methods, the Java platform can distinguish constructors based on the number of arguments included in the lists and their types.

It is not possible for a class to have two constructors with the same name and the same type of arguments since the platform cannot distinguish one from the other; hence encountering a compilation error.

It is not required to have any constructors in a class although caution is advised. It is automatic for the compiler to provide a default constructor without any arguments for a class without constructors. This constructor will invoke the constructor (the constructor without any arguments) of the superclass. During this moment, the compiler will check if the superclass does not have a constructor without arguments so it is important to clarify that it does. (We will discuss more on superclasses and sub-classes after constructors)

Now if a class does not have a declared superclass, it still has a default superclass which contains the default constructor.

Superclasses and Subclasses

```
class MyOwnClass extends MyOwnSuperClass implements MyOwnInterface{
int value;
int result;
}
```

Take a look at the code above. The class MyOwnClass extends another class called MyOwnSuperClass. The MyOwnClass is now called a subclass of MyOwnSuperClass. MyOwnSuperClass is now called the superclass of MyOwnClass. This means that MyOwnClass inherits all the shared attributes and methods of its superclass. Another keyword implement has also been added. The term implement means that the subclass MyOwnClass can use the methods in the class MyOwnInterface. We will discuss more on extends and implements in Inheritance and Interfaces.

It is also possible to add declarations such as public and private at the start.

Overall, a class can have the following components:

- Class modifiers (Public, private, protected)
- Class name
- *if any:

Name of the parent class (superclass) and keyword extends
Note: A subclass can only extend one parent at a time

- Interfaces

-Separated by commas if there are multiple interfaces that need to be implemented

- Class Body

-begins with { and ends with }

Objects

In java, an object is an instance of a class. It is created by the program to interact with everything else through the use of methods. Because of that, a program can carry out multiple objectives such as animation, GUI implementation and information management between a sender and a receiver.

After an object finished its objectives, its resources are again used by other objects.

Methods

We have already introduced ourselves with methods in the previous chapters. As we know, a method is the same as a function in other programming languages like C. It is used to perform specific tasks like calculations and manipulation. Here is an example of a method:

```
public void getAverage (float exam1, float exam2, float exam3){
float average, ex1, ex2, ex3;
average = (ex1 + ex2 + ex3)/3;
System.out.println("The average is: " + average + "%.");
}
```

In a method, the only components needed are the name of the method, the return type, the parameters if there are any, and of course, the body itself.

However, there are some components that can also be added such as modifiers and exception list. Modifiers are important in methods so that data access can be secure and there will be no mishandling of fragile information. Exception lists are also important since they are used in handling runtime errors. More on exception lists to be discussed in the following chapters.

In a method declaration, it is important to always have the method signature. The method signature is the name of the method and its parameter types.

Here is an example:

```
getAverage(float, float, float)
```

Although a method can have any name, it is a good practice for a method name to be a verb in lowercase. If it is a multi-word method name, it is still conventional to start off with a lowercase verb followed by the noun that begins with a capital letter. For example:

getAverage

solveEquation

printAnswer

searchList

isNotEmpty

Method Overloading

Usually, the name of a method is unique within its class. In some cases, however, it is possible for multiple methods in Java to have the same method name. This is called **method overloading.**

In the Java programming language, method overloading is supported. The Java programming language can also determine the difference between methods with different method signatures. In other words, different parameters can determine the difference from one method to the other. Of course, both methods have to be within the same class.

Imagine having a class that can solve 2 numbers of the same datatype. Each method is different for each datatype. It is tiresome to write a new method name for each method. Since Java supports method overloading, it is possible to use the same method name for the multiple methods. The parameters or arguments are the only components that need to be changed.

```
Public class solver{
public void solve ( int a, int b ){ }
public void solve ( float x, float y) { }
public void solve ( double I, double j) { }
}
```

Methods that are overloaded can be distinguished through the number of parameters and the data type passed to the method. If you'll notice in the code above, solve (int a, int b) and solve (float x, float y) clearly have different parameters and are considered different from each other since they require different method parameters.

It is not possible to declare one method with the same name and the same parameters. The compiler will not be able to differentiate them from one another regardless of their body. The Java compiler does not take into consideration the return type of the method when distinguishing them from one another. This means that it is not possible to declare two methods that have the same method signature regardless of their return type.

Method overloading may be a very efficient concept in writing a program, but it reduces the codes readability so its usage is not that often.

Method Value Returning

There are three situations wherein a method exits its section and returns to the main program: First is when the method passes through all the statements in its body Second is when a return statement is encountered, and third, when an exception is thrown.

It is possible to declare the return type of a method in the method declaration. The return statement is then used to return the value of the method evaluated within its body.

If the return type of a method is void, then it does not return any value and it is not required to contain a return statement. However, in some cases, a return statement can be used to manipulate program flow and exit the method—almost similar to a break statement. Trying to return a value from a method with a void declaration will result to a compilation error. On the other hand, if a method is not declared void, it is required to have a return statement with its corresponding value.

It is also vital that the data type of the return value is the same as the data type of the method's declared return type. Take for example trying to return a float value from an integer value. It will result to an error.

```
public int solveAverage ( ) {
return ((score1+score2+score3)/3);
}
```

The method above will return the evaluated value of the expression (score1 + score2 + score3) / 3.

The return statement is not limited to primitive datatypes. It can also return reference type variables. Take a look at the following code:

```
Public MyOwnClass solveMethod( MyOwnClass sample1, myOwnClass sample2) {
MyOwnClass example_1;
//insert some code here
Return example_1;
```

```
}
```

This Statement

We have seen the use of "this" in previous chapters. this actually refers to the current object whose method or constructor is currently being invoked. Through the use of this, it is possible to refer to any member or attribute of the current object from within an instance method.

The this keyword is generally used for a field because it is overshadowed by a method or constructor parameter.

Take a look at the following example:

```
public class sample{
public int a;
public int b;
public sample (int i, int j) {
a = i;
b= j;
}
}
```

Through the use of the this statement, the code can be re-written as:

```
public class sample{
public int a;
public int b;
public sample (int a, int b) {
this.a = a;
this.b = b;
}
}
```

Every argument that the constructor has shadows each of the attributes of the object. The attribute x inside the constructor sample pertains to a local copy of the argument from the class sample. To be able to refer to the sample attribute x, the constructor is required to use this.x.

It is also possible to use the this statement to call another constructor in the same class, provided that it is within a constructor. This process can be called explicit constructor invocation. For example:

```
public class sample {
```

```
private int a, b, var1, var2;
public sample( ) {
this(0, 1, 3, 3);
}
public sample(int var1, int var2) {
this(0, 1, var1, var2);
}
public sample ( int a, int b, int var1, int var2) {
this.a = a;
this.b = b;
this.var1 = var1;
this.var2 = var2;
}
}
```

The code above contains a set of constructors. Each constructor offers a default value and creates instances of the class sample's member variables.

Chapter 5:
Interfaces and Inheritance

In programming and software engineering, there are some scenarios where it is vital for different programmers or different groups of programmers to have a "common ground" that will make their code and software interactive. These programmers should be able to write their code regardless of not knowing how the code of other programmers is written. The "common ground" for these programmers is called an **interface**.

Take for example a community wherein there are advanced vehicles that could operate and transfer people without the help of a human operator. In order for those vehicles to operate, their vehicle manufacturers develop software written in Java that could manipulate the vehicle without human operation. Imagine your vehicle or car starting and accelerating by itself and being able to manage speed to avoid accidents.

Another example that can be considered is the Global Positioning System or GPS. There are computer systems that receive data transmitted by the GPS in order to track the location of a vehicle and provide wireless transmission of other data such as up-to-date maps, weather and traffic situations. Together with GPS, automated vehicles can have a sense of which route to choose the correct direction in order to get to a destination without having any hassle such as traffic.

Now the GPS software and automation software for the vehicle are clearly made by different teams of programmers. The team of programmers who developed the automation software does not have any idea what the code of the GPS software looks like or how it is implemented but they can interact with each other through a single common ground. That is the interface. Each team of programmers can actually have their code modified by the other team as long as they keep the interactivity of the interface.

Java Interfaces

The Java programming languages addresses an interface as a reference type. It is considered similar to a class which can only contain constants, default and static methods, method signatures and nested class types. The method bodies of an interface are included only for the purpose of default and static methods.

An interface cannot have an instance. It is not possible to instantiate an interface as it can only be implemented or extended by classes or other interfaces.

Here is an example of an interface:

```
Public interface automateVehicle {
//static variable declarations
// method signatures
int init(Speed s, float distance, float gas, float angle, boolean collision);
int accelerate (Speed s, float gas, float distance);
int decelerate (Speed s, float gas, float distance, boolean collision) ;
int steerWheel (Speed s, float distance, boolean collision);
//other methods
}
```

Note: Remember that method signatures do not require curly braces as they are terminated by a semi-colon.

In order to use an interface, the keyword *implements* is used. Whenever a class that can be instantiated implements an interface, it creates a method body for the methods declared in the interface.

The following code is an example:

```
Public class Car implements automateVehicle {
Int init (Speed s, float distance, float gas, float angle, boolean collision)
//the code above contains the method signatures and the implementation
//code to make the class car init goes here
// some more code
}
//other class members can be written here
}
```

If you remembered, the developers of the interface automateVehicle are not the same developers of the class car. Other car classes can use the automateVehicle interface and have a different implementation from the other but both still need to keep the same interface. These car developers will then build systems such as GPS systems and digital maps and make them usable and effective through the use of the methods of the interface.

The interface automateVehicle example shows the use of the interface in the real world as an *Application Programming Interface* (API). APIs can also be found in other software products. Usually, a software package that contains methods that other companies could use for their own product is developed and sold by another company as well.

Take for example two companies: one graphics company an one software company. The graphics company develops the classes to implement the interface. The software company then uses the interface developed by the graphics company for their own software. Although the interface API of the software company is for sale and available to the public, the implementation remains kept in secret. It is actually possible that the implementation of the API be revised in the future as long as the interest and use for the public remains efficient.

Interface Declaration and Definition

There are five components that an interface needs to be declared: the modifier, the interface name, list of parent interfaces it there are any, the body, and the keyword interface, of course.

```
    public    interface    SampleInterface    extends    AnotherInterface,    ThatInterface,
SampleInterfaceAgain {
    float value = 1.54;
    void doSomething (int i, double x);
    int doSomethingElse(String s);}
```

In the previous code, the modifier public means that other classes from any package can gain access to the interface. If the modifier of the interface is not specified, the interface, by default, will only be accessible to the classes within the same package.

Like a regular class, it is possible to extend interfaces. It can't just extend one class; it can extend any number of interfaces, hence the list of parent interfaces that it extends if there are any.

Now, the body of the interface can contain multiple methods such as abstract methods, default methods and static methods. Each method is a bit different from the other.

An abstract method is almost the same as a method signature. It does not need implementation. A default method is a method which is declared within the default modifier. A static modifier, on the other hand, is declared within the static modifier. The abstract, static and default methods within an interface are by default, public.

Besides the methods, it is also possible to use constant declarations in interfaces. Every constant value declared in an interface can be any of the modifiers (public, static, final).

For a class to be able to implement an interface, the keyword implements must be written before the interface name in the declaration. It is possible for a class to implement more than one interface. If that situation happens, the interfaces to be implemented by the class are separated by commas. If a class is extending a superclass and implements an interface, the keyword extends is always followed by the superclass name, and then the implements keyword.

Imagine an interface that defines a comparison between sizes of objects:

```
public interface Comparison{
public int isSmallerThan(Comparison object_1);
}
```

In order to be able to compare the sizes of similar objects regardless of their type, the interface Comparison needs to be implemented by the class that instantiates them.

It is possible for any class to implement the interface Comparison as long as there is a method that can compare the similar field of objects that are instantiated from the class. For other datatypes such as strings, the number of characters can be compared. For other objects such as person, fields such as height and age can be used. For mathematical situations such geometrical objects, areas can have comparisons while other situations such as volume would be suitable for three-dimensional object comparisons. The method isSmallerThan() can be implemented by all the said classes.

If it is known that a class can implement the interface Comparison, then it is also a fact that it is possible to compare the object size instantiated from its class.

Inheritance

We have seen the application of inheritance in some of the previous chapters. The Java programming language allows classes to be derived from other classes. With that being possible, the attributes and methods of the parent class will be inherited by the derived class or the subclass.

The following code is a simple implementation of the class Vehicle which was used in an earlier example:

```
Public class Car implements automateVehicle {
public class Vehicle {
Float distance;
Float gas;
Float angle;
public Vehicle(float Vgas, float Vdistance, float Vangle ) {
gas = Vgas;
distance = Vdistance;
angle = Vangle;
}
Public void setDistance(int Ndistance){
distance = Ndistance;
}
public void setGas(int Ngas) {
gas = Ngas;
}
Public void turnStraight(int value){
angle-= value;
}
Public void turn(int value){
Angle+= value;
```

```
}
}
```

The class declaration for class Car that is a subclass of class **Vehicle** will look like this:

```
public class Car extends Vehicle {
public int heatRate;
public Car(float heatR, float sDistance, float sGas, float sAngle) {
super(sDistance, sGas, sAngle);
heatRate = heatR;
}
// the car subclass adds one method
public void setHeatRate(int newValue) {
heatRate = newValue;
}
}
```

The subclass Car gets to inherit all the fields and methods of its superclass Vehicle. It also adds another method named setHeatRate and its field heatRate. Besides the constructor, writing the subclass Vehicle seems like it was a different class made entirely from nothing, together with its fields and methods. That was how it felt but now how it was made. This technique will be very important if the methods in the superclass Vehicle were more complex and took a very long time to debug.

A subclass is a class derived from another class. It can also be called a derived class, or child class. The opposite of the subclass is the superclass. A superclass is the class where the subclass was derived. Another term for a superclass is the parent class.

All the members from the superclass, including the attributes, methods, and other nested classes, are inherited by the subclass. Although it does not inherit the constructors but the constructor of the superclass can be called from the subclass.

The Java Programming Language does not support multiple superclass inheritance. This means that every class can only have one direct superclass. Besides an object, every class is basically a subclass of

Object; Assuming that the said class does not have a declared superclass. A subclass having a subclass extended by another subclass is possible. The topmost superclass of every class is the class Object. Every single class can be traced back to object regardless of the subclasses.

The concept of inheritance can be very efficient when it comes to handling multiple classes that basically have the same structure.

For example, imagine a class Mountain and class Valley. Instead of rewriting all the attributes of class Mountain to class Valley, it is possible to create a class Landform which contains all the same attributes and methods that both class Mountain and class Valley have. This also reduces the possibility of errors and reduces debugging time.

Java Platform Hierarchy

In the Java Programming Language, the class Object is basically the core class of all classes. It is the most common of all classes. All classes are derived from class Object. These classes then can have subclasses and so on. This is called a hierarchy of classes. Classes at the bottom of the hierarchy tend to perform more specific methods compared to their superclasses.

Subclasses

A subclass can inherit all the public and protected members of its parent regards less of what package the subclass is located in. If both the subclass and its parent are in the same package, the subclass can also inherit all of the parent's private members. With that said, a subclass can do manipulations to its inherited members such as:

- Direct usage of the inherited fields
- Declaring a field within the subclass but having the same name as the superclass
- Declaring new fields not included in the superclass
- Direct usage of all the inherited methods from the parent
- Creating a new instance method in the subclass that can have the same method signature in the superclass (method

overriding)

- Creating a new static method with the same name as the superclass
- Declaring new methods in the subclass that are not included in the superclass
- Creating a subclass constructor that calls the constructor of the superclass

A subclass cannot inherit the private members of its parent class. This can only be possible if both the subclass and the parent class are in the same package.

If the methods used by the superclass for accessing private fields are either public or protected, these methods are accessible to the subclass. The nested classes in a class have access to all of the private fields and methods of its enclosing class. Hence, if a nested class is either public or protected, its subclass gains access to all of the private members of its superclass.

We have already discussed that the object is from the data type of the class where it was instantiated. For example:

```
public MyOwnClass sample = new MyOwnClass ( );
```

The data type of the object sample is MyOwnClass.

The object sample comes from the class MyOwnClass. This makes sample a MyOwnClass and also an object which can be used for all the purposes of MyOwnClass or Object.

The idea that MySuperClass maybe a MyOwnClass may be true is not necessary. It can be considered the same as an Object can be a MySuperClass or MyOwnClass is true but not necessary.

The use of an object of one type as a substitute or alternative for another type among the list of objects where inheritance and implementation are possible is called Casting.

For example:

```
Object obj1 = new MyOwnClass ( );
```

The code above declares that obj1 is declared as both an Object and a MyOwnClass. This method is called implicit casting.

The following code, on the other hand is called explicit casting:

```
MyOwnClass sample = obj1;
    MyOwnClass sample = (MyOwnClass) obj;
```

If the type MyOwnClass was not assigned to obj1, the code would have encountered an error since the datatype of obj1 was originally unknown. Explicit casting initializes an observation during runtime to make sure that obj1 is of the type MyOwnClass. This is to ascertain that the compiler can identify obj1 is an instance of MyOwnClass. If obj1 does not become an instance of MyOwnClass, the program throws out an exception.

It is possible to determine the type of a particular object using "instanceof". This reduces the chances of encountering a runtime error due to an improper cast.

```
    if (obj1 instanceof MMyOwnClass) {
    MyOwnClass sample = (MyOwnClass) obj1;
    }
```

The instanceof operator checks if obj1 refers to MyOwnClass in order to make the cast without the possibility of having a thrown runtime exception.

Multiple Inheritance

The difference between classes and interfaces is that interfaces are not allowed to have fields while classes can. Another difference is that an interface cannot make an instance of itself to create an object while a class can be instantiated to create one. As discussed in chapter 4, objects can store their current state in fields which can be defined through the use of classes.

The reason why the Java Programming Language does not allow a class to have more than one super class is to avoid the possibility of multiple inheritance of the state, or in other words, the ability to inherit fields from multiple classes.

Consider a situation where it is possible to create a class that can extend multiple classes. When an object is created through an instance of a class, the fields of all of the superclass of that class will be inherited by the object. There will be a possibility that a method or constructor can create an instance of the same fields. This will be very difficult to resolve. This is also why interfaces cannot contain fields; to avoid the problems from multiple inheritance of state.

The ability to inherit method definitions from multiple classes is called multiple inheritance of implementation. This type of inheritance can have a lot of problems such as conflicts with method names. Programming languages that are able to support multiple inheritance of implementation might encounter situations such as multiple superclasses that have methods of the same names. The compilers of these programming languages will not be able to distinguish the difference of one method from the other. Human errors such as creating a conflict with the methods of a superclass can also happen.

Default methods also have a different form of multiple inheritance of implementation. Multiple interfaces can be implemented by more a class. These interfaces can contain default methods with the same name. In Java, the compiler has rules that could verify the default method a particular class needs or uses.

The Java Programming Language has the capability to support multiple inheritance of type. This is technically the ability to implement more than one interface. It is possible for an object to have multiple types. These types can be of types of their own class or the types of all the interfaces implemented by the class. In other words, if a declared variable is declared as a type of an interface, the value of that variable can be used to reference any instantiated object from any class where the interface is being implemented.

Multiple inheritance of implementation, on other hand, allows a class to inherit different implementations from an interface that it extends any method defined.

Instance Method

In a subclass, an instance method with the same signature and return type as an instance method in a superclass has the capability to override the instance method of the superclass.

Due to the overriding ability of a subclass, a class can be allowed to inherit from a superclass whose characteristics are relatively similar and modify those characteristics as required. The components (name, type and number of parameters, return type) of the overriding method must be the same as the method that it will override. It is also possible for an overriding method to return the subtype of the type returned by the overridden method; In other words, a *covariant return type*.

During method overriding, it is recommended to use the @Override so that the compiler will be instructed that a method in the superclass will be overridden. If the method to be overridden in the superclass does not exist, an error will occur.

Static Methods

When an identical static method (identical method signatures) from a superclass is defined within a subclass, the method from the subclass will hide the method from the superclass.

The difference between instance method overriding and static method overriding are:

- The overridden instance method in the subclass is the method that is invoked.
- The hidden static method that gets used may vary since the location where it is invoked may vary between a superclass and a subclass.

In an interface, default methods and abstract methods can be treated like instance methods in such a way that they can be inherited like instance methods. Although if the supertypes of a class or interface already have default methods with the same method signatures, the java compiler will follow the rules of inheritance so that the conflict in method name will be resolved. These rules are:

- Interface default methods are less preffered over instance methods.
- Overriden methods by other candidates will be ignored. This situation happens when the supertypes have a similar ancestor.
- In the case of abstract methods, if there is at least one defined default method that conflicts with an abstract method, a compiler error will be thrown by the Java compiler. It is important to note that the supertype methods must be overridden explicitly.

Polymorphism

In Biology, the term polymorphism is referred to where in an organism or species can assume multiple different phases or forms. In the Java programming language, this concept is also applicable. The unique behaviors can be defined by their own subclass but still be able to share some of the similar functionalities of the parent class.

To be able to demonstrate polymorphism, we will make some adjustments to the class Vehicle. For example, a method named displayData can be added to the class. This method displays all the data that are currently stored in an instance.

```
public void displayData( ){
    System.out.println("\nThe Vehicle is " + "in the correct" + this.
    + " with a gas in liters of " + this.gas +
    " and currently have a total distance travelled of " + this.distance + ". ");
    }
```

To be able to demonstrate the features of polymorphism in the Java Programming Language, the class Vehicle is extended by a class Car and a RallyCar class. For the class Car, a field named breaks will be added, which is a String value that indicates if the car contains a back shock absorber, Here is the updated class:

```java
public class Car extends Vehicle {
private String breaks;
public Car(
int sDistance,
int sGas,
int sAngle,
String breakType){
super(sDistance
sGas,
sAngle);
this.setBreaks(breakType);
}
public String getBreaks(){
return this.breaks;
}
```

```java
public void setBreaks(String breakType) {
    this.break = breakType;
    }
    public void displayData( ) {
    super.displayData();
    System.out.println("The " + "car has a" +
    getBreaks( ) + " type as breaks");
    }
    }
```

Notice the overridden method displayData. Another detail to be considered is the data about the breaks that is included in the ouput.

The next step is to create the RallyCar class. Since Rally cars use different sets of wheels to be able to turn in dirt, a new field WheelWidth has been added to the set of fields. Here is the RallyCar class:

```
public class RallyCar extends Vehicle{
private int WheelWidth;
public RallyCar(int sDistance,
int sGas,
int sAngle,
int newWheelWidth){
super(startDistance,
startGas,
startAngle);
this.setWheelWidth(newWheelWidth);
}


public int getWheelWidth(){
    return this.WheelWidth;
    }
    public void setWheelWidth(int newWheelWidth){
    this.WheelWidth = newWheelWidth;
    }
    public void displayData(){
    super.displayData();
    System.out.println("The Rally Car" + " has " + getWheelWidth() +
    "set of wheels.");
    }
    }
```

The Java virtual machine (JVM) has the ability to call the appropriate method for the object that is being referred to in each variable. It does not have the capability to call a method that is defined by the type of the variable. This characteristic can be referred to as virtual method invocation. This demonstrates an aspect of the vital features of poly-morphism in the Java Programming Language.

Chapter 6:
Packages

In programming, developers tend to group related types into groups so that they can be easier to find and to avoid conflicts in names. These groups are called packages.

A package is basically a group of related types that allow access protection and management of name space.

Note: Remember that a type can be referred to as a class, interface, annotation, or enumeration.

The special kinds of classes are enumerations while the special kinds of interfaces are called annotations, but generally, types are usually referred to as classes and interfaces.

In the Java Platform, there are types that are also members of some packages that can group a class by function. For example:

Java.lang contains the fundamental classes while java.io contains the classes used for reading and writing (input / output). There are other packages that provide other functions than i/o and fundamental functions. It is also possible for a programmer to bundle their classes into a package.

The advantages of grouping classes and interfaces into packages are:

- It is convenient and more accessible for other programmers to locate specific types such as graphics-related functions.
- There won't be a conflict in type names and the name of the types developed since a package utilizes the use of a new namespace.
- Unrestricted access is possible between types within the same package but retain protected access from types from other packages.

Package Creation

In creating a package, it is important to first choose a name and precede it with a package statement wherein the name must be written at the top of every source file that contains the types you wish to include from and in the package.

Take for example:

Package example;

The line of code above needs to be the first line to be written in a source file. A maximum of one package statement can only be written per source file. This rule applies to all types in the file.

If multiple types are places in a single source file, only one type can be modified to public. That name of that type must also be the same as the name of the source file.

Take for example a source file named Test.java and Example.java, It is possible to define a public class named Test in the file. It is also possible to define a public interface named Example in the source file Example.java. The exclusivity of the type name to the source file is important.

Non-public types can also be included in the same file by being treated as a public type although this practice is not recommended unless the size of the non-public type is small and relatively close to the public type. Non-public types can be included but the access to the public type will only be available from outside of the package. This means that all top-level, non-public types will remain private within the package.

Whenever a graphics interface and classes that implanting the graphics interface in a package called graphics, a total of six source files will be needed.

If the package statement is not used, the type will end up in an unnamed package. An unnamed package is usually used for small and temporary applications only or used as form early development stages of a program. If your type is important, then it should be put in a named package.

Since there are now so many programmers in the whole world developing classes and interfaces with the Java Programming Language, there is a high probability that a lot of programmers will use the name for different types.

Conventions in Naming Packages

Package names are normally written in lower case letters to avoid the possibility of conflict with class names or interface names.

Packages names used by companies usually come from their domain names but are reversed. For example:

net.sample.samplepackage

The packages in the Java Programming Language, Java Language to be precise, begin with the work java. or in some cases, javax.

There are some situations where in using the domain name is not a valid package name. This situation can occur if the name of the domain contains a symbol or a special character like '@'. It will also be invalid if the package name begins with a number or any character that should not be used. A package name will also be invalid if the name begins with special keywords such as int. The safest symbol to use is a simple name which can be followed by an underscore.

Package member usage

The components inside a package are usually called package members. In order to use a package member (public) from the outside, referring to a member by its full name can be done. Importing the package member itself is also possible. Another way is importing the entire package where the member comes from. These solutions can be applied to specific situations.

Name referral is probably the most used way of referring to a member or method or type that we have seen from the previous chapters. It is possible to utilize the simple name of a package member if both the code being developed and the package member are from the same package or the package member itself was imported.

Although this method is useful, it needs to utilize the fully qualified name of the member including the package name when trying to use a member from a different package that has not been imported.

Fully qualified names are used for non-frequent moments. A name used multiple times can become tiresome and makes the code difficult to understand so importing the member or the package itself is done as a simpler solution.

Package Member Import

To be able to import a member into a current file, add the import statement at the beginning of the file before everything else but not before the package statement if one is being used.

Package Import

To be able to import all the components within a package, use the same method as importing package members but use an asterisk instead of the member name. This imports all the members instead of just one.

The asterisk character can only be used to specify that all classes within the package are being imported. It cannot be used to match a specific member or subset within the package. This will make the compiler throw a compilation error. The import statement specifies that either a single member or the entire package can be imported. The import statement has another form that allows public nested classes of an enclosing class to be imported.

Packages may seem hierarchical but they are not. The order at which packages are imported does not have any effect on how the members and types are used within the program.

Ambiguity

If there are two members from different packages that share a common name, these members need to be imported through the use of fully qualified name method. This is done to avoid any ambiguity between the names from different packages.

The Static Import Statement

In importing packages, there are some cases where in access to fields and a static method from more than one class is frequent. Using the class names as a prefix multiple times will lead to an unreadable code that can be very difficult to understand.

The static import statement allows a solution for importing the static methods and constants that are needed to avoid the multiple prefix problems.

Source and Class File Management

The Java Programming Language platform has many implementations that rely on hierarchical file systems in order to be able to manage class and source files although this is not required in the Java Language Specification. To be able to do this, the following steps must be done:

Place the source code for a type in a text file whose name is the name of type and with a file extension of .java.

```
//from a file called sample.java
Package example;
Public class sample{
//code
}
```

After that, put the source file in a directory whose name is the same name as the package name of where it belongs.

The names of the package members and the path name to the files should be parallel. Assuming the file name separator is backslash (Microsoft Windows).

As we have discussed from previous topics, it is a common practice that a package name is derived from its company's domain name. Remember the example domain name sample.net will have its package name as net.sample. All the components inside the package will correspond to a sub-directory. So if the company of the domain sample.net has a package member named net.sample.packagemember that contains a file sample.java, it will be placed in a series of subdirectories such as:

```
....\net\sample\package\sample.java
```

When compiling a source file, a different output file is created by the compiler for each type defined.

Wrapping Up

Overall, the Java Programming Language is a very powerful programming language that can be used in many aspects. Having goals such as being simple, object-oriented, independent of the host platform, the ability to contain language facilities and libraries for network systems and a structure specifically designed to have code be executed securely from remote source, the Java programming language has features that are not present in other programming languages like C and C++.

Considering the modularity of the Java programming language, its capability to divide codes into modules gives it a tremendous advantage over other languages such as C/C ++. In Java, the output application can be drawn out in the form of modules instead of just a single executable. Programming languages like C/C++ on the other hand, when encountering small changes or adjustments in code, require the whole application to be recompiled.

The idea of the Java Programming Language is to be able to compile a source code into an intermediate language that can be interpreted. The intermediate language is considered the byte code. While the Java Virtual Machine or JVM is the interpreter. In terms of Standardization, Java has standardized libraries which have the ability to gain access to features of host machines such as network and graphics in multiple ways. The Java programming language can also support multi-threaded programs which can be necessary for networking applications.

Java is also platform independent and will be even more powerful and efficient when tagged with server side applications such web services and mini servers. For the client side, Java has also provided some improvements such as Windows toolkits, widget toolkits, and Swing. Java is a write once, run anywhere programming language. This means that there are not that many problems with its portability to any hardware as long as there is a Java Virtual Machine present. It is also a write once, test anywhere programming language. This makes Java very efficient and fast.

For execution and error handling, Java can make an exception throw an object just like any other object. The only requirement it needs is to implement the interface Throwable. The compiler also specifies whether or not an exception may be caught. If there is not catch block made for a thrown exception. The compiler will produce an error.

Java forces its programmers to handle exceptions. With that said, the programmer must be able to handle the exception or define that the user must be able to handle it.

In the field of networking capabilities, the predecessors of Java did not have a feature that could allow their language to network with other computer systems. This means they became platform independent and almost all network protocols are standardized. This made the developers of the Java language add more focus on its integration in the Internet.

Java was originally designed with networking computing as one of its features. It was one of the first language systems to offer wide support for a code from a remote source execution.

For dynamic class loading, classes in Java can be compiled as needed. If a class is not required during the execution of a program, it is impossible to compile the class into code.

This perk is highly useful when it comes to networking programming. Being able to run a program that could load classes from the file system or remote source is a very efficient concept. It can also be possible for a program written in Java Language to alter its own code while being in an execution. However, it is more realistic and possible for a program written in Java to be executed with some feedback and improve the generated code over time.

In Java, releasing the memory is no longer in the programmer's list of responsibilities. The Java Virtual Machine (jvm) keeps track of and records all the used memory. When a memory is not used anymore, it automatically freed up. While that is happening, another task is being done in the background by JVM: releasing up unreferenced, unused memory which can also be called Garbage Collection. The garbage collector is always running. This feature makes it easy to write complex server side programs. The only thing the programmer has to do now is to observe the speed of the creation of the object. If an application is creating objects faster than the Garbage Collector can free, this will cause memory problems. The application may either run out of memory or throw out an exception, or halt to give time for the Garbage Collector to keep up and do its tasks.

One more thing that can be said about Java is that the people behind it were also the creators of the concept of the applet. A Java program has the capability to be run in a web browser. Java was originally designed for web applications. The promise of the Java programming language was in the web browser side and that the code could be downloaded and executed as an applet for the browser.

Since Java is basically an upgrade of some programming languages, there were some features in the other languages that were disabled such as multiple inheritance, restrictions of typecasting and many more in Java to avoid errors.

As a final generalization, Java is a programming language that can deliver results and live up to its goals. The Java language is not just some other language as it allows the creation of advanced data types (objects) which can be representations of real-world things. These objects can have fields that can be modified as well.

Java is a very flexible programming language. From the development of software to the development of applets as well; java has proven to be a powerful language in many aspects. But its flexibility is not yet over. Since it is platform independent, the same Java programs can be run on various operating systems with having the need to recreate or rewrite the code, unlike programming languages like C and C++. This was all possible due because of the Java Runtime Environment which interprets the Java source code and relays the operating system on what needs to be done.

Of course, the language has some drawbacks, but it is still easy to understand and learn. In a span of one day, any person can be able to create their own Java programs.